Pass It On

Larry L. Wallace

ISBN 979-8-88540-361-0 (paperback)
ISBN 979-8-88540-362-7 (digital)

Christian Faith Publishing
832 Park Avenue
Meadville, PA 16335
www.christianfaithpublishing.com

Printed in the United States of America

Acknowledgments

This is the knowledge that I have received from the Grand Master Howard Woods. During one Grand Session, I attempted to thank him for the knowledge that he had shared with me over the years that I had been in masonry. He said, "If you want to thank me, Pass It On." So, I will attempt to give you what I received from him.

These first few writings are verbatim as Grand Master Woods wrote them, which is titled "Freemasonry" and is written in six parts. We will start with Part 1.

The Apprentice

In every lodge, in every chapter of Royal Arch Masons, in every commandery of Knights Templar, in every consistory of princes and peers, in every temple of Nobles, in every appendant body of Freemasonry, you'll find him, the Master Mason.

He did not start out that way. He approached a member of the lodge. The lodge voted to accept him. He was initiated into the mysteries that he found not to be a mystery at all, just mysterious. As the master mason found himself among other brothers of the craft, he saw and found out about the strength of friendship, the value of it, and the necessity of it. He was made aware of scriptures he had already read in his life but without a deeper understanding. He found out that Freemasonry did not seek to replace his own religious beliefs, but it did seek to compliment them. He was in a learning stage of Freemasonry, a throwback to his childhood when he went to school and, of times, when the whys and hows were foremost in his young mind. The apprenticed mason remembers the early years of his life, the formative years, years when he was indeed inquisitive and was asked by the lodge to continue seeking.

The apprenticed mason was caused to disavow all the superficial trappings of meaningless life but to hold fast to those things that were of a more permanent nature, things like morality and spirituality. He was taken through ancient worlds of man, showing him that

there is a common denominator in all religions, the belief in God. In these worlds, he was caused to study the life of people, God's greatest and last creations. He was taken through avenues of history in order to understand the relationships of men and God through different names for Him, different ideas about Him.

The apprenticed mason learned the noblest entity on earth, work, and all its branches. Work was shown to be a true enemy to Satan, the master of idleness. Work was shown to enrich the mind as well as the physical being. He was given tools to work with, tools that taught as well as providing ways of accomplishment. The lessons gained from the working tools were philosophical and meaningful in spirit and in actuality. The apprenticed mason was taught that if he did not work, there would be no rewards here or in any future period.

The mason was given rules and guides to live by, to coexist by, and to be gauged by. He soon found that all the rules he ever needed were found in the greatest light before him, the Volume of the Sacred Law. But because of man's frailties, explanations were necessary for man's enlightenment. He found out about allegories, parables in another time, and how they put absolute truths before him, complex in hearing and sight but simple in understanding. He found out that truth is "like a shadow in the night"—illusive yet attainable. The rules and regulations diminish, for he is allowed to dwell in a spiritual world where there are only two rules: Love of God and Love of Man. The apprenticed mason is caused to receive gifts like a lambskin apron; the emblem of innocence and purity, which the heart should be; modes of recognition so that he may know other brothers of the craft even though they be strangers; words; signs; and grips. The mason is accepted among the craft because of friendship extraordinaire, friends of friends. His continued existence as a brother mason will hinge on his remaining friendly. Otherwise, he will become just a member of the Masonic fraternity, never to know the beauty of the "tie that binds."

The apprenticed mason goes to school—schools of instructions, schools of life—as he meanders through his community of city, invested with certain keys that will unlock the doors, and he can enter into the world of further light. The mason is brought face-to-face as to what manhood is all about. As he learns by conversing with well-informed brethren, manhood is attained through his inquisitive mind, not through his experienced body.

The Apprentice

The Entered Apprenticed Mason is put in the care of a fellowcraft mason, like a "big brother" system. Big brother is to teach the apprentice the way to live by working at his trade, being an upright man, and finding God in all walks of the apprentice's life. The apprentice enters into a world heretofore unknown to him.

A picture is worth a thousand words; and God, in His infinite wisdom, gave us untold thousands of pictures, scenes that were placed here on earth even before the creation of man. God gave us the patterns of the universe when He gave to us the lesser creations that He made in the time before man. From these creations, God showed us how, when, what, and where. In so doing, He also covered all lessons with a cloak of simplicity, knowing all along that man would seek answers through complexities rather than through the simple things in life. The apprentice learns of the basics, the simplicities, the normal, and the answerable. The apprentice is an empty cup, and the fellowcraft mason has but to fill it with good and wholesome work.

The apprentice must have a hearty appetite for knowledge, for this is the forerunner of wisdom. He is to actively seek to occupy his time in the attainment of not only knowledge but useful knowledge. Around him are lessons to be gained from nature herself. In her bosom, a never-ending fountain is waiting to be tapped, and the fellowcraft mason is there to help the apprentice unlock the doors

that bar his way to understanding. In the fellow's mind and in his hands are tools to accomplish this task, tools that show the uninitiated only superficial explanations. The rule becomes a gauge, the hammer a gavel of divestment. In both, the apprentice learns of time and weaknesses.

From the hammer, the apprentice learns divestments, divesting his mind and his conscience of all impurities. This must be done before the apprentice can do anything for anyone else. Jesus put in a very simple form, "Get the mote from your own eye before you attempt to remove it from others." Too often, the apprentice had found himself in a judging position, setting himself up over the rest of his brothers and sisters. The hammer, or common gavel, causes the brick or stone to change its image; likewise, the apprentice is changed if he adheres to the lesson of the divestments.

The apprentice learns from his brothers and fellows, for they are the examples. Therefore, the brothers and fellows owe the apprentice a true example of who and what they are in the patterns of life. As the apprentice is the seeker, the brothers and fellows then should become the sought-after. If the apprentice is seeking a recommendation, give it. If he asks for a commendation, advance it. If he knocks upon the door of your experience, share it. He has nowhere else to turn, for he is just a stone, just out of the quarry of life, and the brother and/or the fellow with the tools is the one responsible for erecting a temple on this cornerstone. What kind of temple will be determined in the fulfillment of the apprentice's life, whether his work will be accepted or rejected?

The Fellowcraft

Forty-two thousand Ephraimites lost their heads because they couldn't give the right word. Many men have started out on the journey toward the completion of the master mason's degree and lost their heads (mentally) and, like the Ephraimites, died on the way—a mental and intellectual death to be sure but a death that shouldn't have happened.

A fellowcraft mason represents a man, full grown, one that stands upright before God and man in several ways. He is a man that has come through the valley of decision and has made the choice that all men must make: which way to go.

The essential learning days have passed away, and a fellowcraft must stand on his actions rather than his words. His life is mute testimony to the glory or lack of glory of his thoughts toward God and the fraternity. It is his now to present his work for pay, and a good worker is worthy of his hire. The tools of the entered apprenticed mason are added to the tools of the fellowcraft, and at once he becomes a doer as well as a teacher.

At the building of King Solomon's temple, there were more fellowcraft masons than there were apprentices. That holds true today on any construction job that you see. In real life, there should be more men than boys, but alas, that is not always the case.

A fellowcraft mason—good fellowcraft mason—takes time and tries to do the job right, for his mark will go on it. His work will be accepted or rejected on its uprightness, leveling, and squaring, just as his life will be judged by the same principles on that Great Judgment Day. Who will pass inspections is given to only the Father, but I am sure that everyone that works in the quarry will know, somehow, which way he will go. A man knows when his work is worthy!

A fellowcraft is called a journeyman today, and possibly, not too many know the reason why. It is simple. As a fellowcraft, which means that he is qualified to do the work, the mason is entitled to receive wages when the apprentice has not received his keep and only got the bare necessities of life. Such is the journeyman today. He can work for any master at any time as long as he is licensed to do so.

A fellowcraft mason learns further of the several signs and symbols of the order and lives by the lessons derived from them. He is taught the five senses of human life and parallels them with the five orders of architecture that he finds representing human life and societies: three originals and two bastards.

He learns that of the human senses, these are required for membership in the order those of seeing, hearing and feeling, extensions of seeking, asking, and knocking. As he receives his working tools, he learns of the importance of the teaching of Amos, the country preacher. He learns of the importance of treating everyone right in everyday business. He also learns of equality before God who is no respecter of persons, but rather we find ourselves on the same level in all our travels.

The fellowcraft teaches the apprentice well so that the apprentice will not necessarily stumble in life; but if he should, he can pick himself up when he is able and expect help when he can't. The fellowcraft makes his obligation and then lives up to it, knowing that a man's word is his bond, for he now knows that the Word has gone man's bond. While as an apprentice, he learned of morality. He now learns intellect, the training of the rhythm that exist between the

mind and the body, creating two out of the three principal supports of the lodge that of Wisdom and Strength. Beauty will come later.

The fellowcraft mason: One who stands upright, acts squarely, and travels on a level.

The Fellowcraft

The fellowcraft mason makes a return visit to King Solomon's temple by a way that he had not traveled before. As he travels, he learns of things of an earthly nature, things that he must do if he is to progress higher to a spiritual level. His learning days are not over even though he has passed to the fellowcraft stage in the fraternity. But now, considering what he has learned, he must use what he has.

What does he have? That is the question! In his mind, there must be a thousand ways that he would like to use what he has, which is a great awareness of life as a juvenile would view life after graduation from high school. His tools are different as his work is different. The lessons of the tool of the fellowcraft follow the same direction as the tools of the apprenticed mason, upward in thought. He has been taught about morality, so his plumb teaches him to be an upright man, standing tall in his community, in his home, his church, his job. He has learned that, if a man does not stand for something, he will fall for anything! Therefore, his life is no longer the private property he has assumed but a vehicle to be used by being of service to mankind. The square that he has received teaches him how to treat his fellowman in transacting any kind of business on the square. As he learns of the spiritual nature of the things around him, he comes to the realization that all are traveling on the "same level of time…"

As he learns and puts into practice what he has learned, the fellowcraft finds out that he must return to his temple for further instructions. The instruction he has received thus far is great but hardly sufficient to understand the universe that has just been portrayed to him. The lessons he has learned are hardly sufficient to truly contemplate the wonder of God's creations. Therefore, he must return to the temple.

Man, in his quest for knowledge and wisdom of a necessity, must return to the training ground. "Take me back, take me back, take me back where I first believed" goes the famous song heard in African American communities. In the same vein, the fellowcraft is taken back to the same temple but to a different level. While traveling through the lower levels, he sees his life in three stages: one of learning, one of doing, and one of remembering. The fellowcraft sees his very being compared with the architecture, man's documents of history in stone. He finds out about the seven liberal arts and sciences and their applications. Then he arrives to the place where he comes face-to-face with rewards, for he is paid his wages, those of nourishment, refreshment, and joy.

In his return flights, the fellowcraft glimpses the ultimate goal when he is shown the terrestrial and celestial globes. The lesson stands out "that if you want to get up, you must get down." In his joy for having reached this plateau and to get a glimpse of the lodge of Adam and Eve, he is reminded of the pillars at the entrance and how, "in this house, shall strength be established." He learns that the strength of purpose is not the character that establishes a covenant with his Creator. But the strength of the covenant that the Creator has established with those that would follow after Him. Little does the fellowcraft know that he is in the area of the Logos, the creative force by which the world was made and that, if he is to ascend to the higher heights of life, he must master the terrestrial before he can enjoy the celestial.

The fellowcraft returns to the temple again and again, each time seeking, asking until, finally, he is to stand in the presence of masters, those that have mastered the "work." In time, he will take his place with the adepts, the illuminated ones, but for now, the temple waits

and instructs the winding stairs to remain stable, waiting for the fellowcraft to ascent and descend them, receiving wages, and being of
service. As he has returned to the temple again and again, so does
his mind return to the simple things he has observed: silence and
strength before the adversities of life, instructions when ignorance
abounds, fidelity when betrayal is easier.

The Highest Degree

The fellowcraft mason has been notified: be at the lodge hall for the raising of candidates; graduation is at hand. Excitement must have traveled through the fellowcraft's heart as "this is it!" He is about to become a master mason, the highest degree in Freemasonry!

In the first degree, the candidate is taught morality, the difference between right and wrong, and more importantly, how to apply it in his everyday life. The lesson was not meant to undermine any teaching the candidate has received from his church, temple, or synagogue, but rather to act as a reminder of what was taught. In the lodge, the same lessons are put before him, lessons to be lived, lessons to be learned all over again but with particular meanings.

In the second degree, the candidate was taught how to discharge the duties that he owes to God, neighbor, and self. He is taught how to teach others what he has been taught as with the fellowcraft and entered apprentice masons of old. He is taught how to learn and then teach by doing, rather than talking about it. He is taught how to apply his lessons in a small group, thereby preparing for the larger group that he will face in everyday life.

Now he is to become a master mason, one to attempt to master all of what he has been taught and experienced. Being called a master mason does not mean that he will necessarily make the grade, but it does mean that he will be in a position to learn what other masters

have learned. Many times in his life, this lesson will come back to him that all cannot be master mason even though they may be in position to be such. The master mason's degree is not for everyone, and consequently, disappointment may overcome the many that seek and don't find. Yet a man must be in search of the quest, the goal of enlightenment. As the master said, "He that hath an ear, let him hear."

Our degrees are structured so that each member may eat of the Masonic meal, each to his own appetite. What is a full meal for most is but an appetizer for a few. To master the field of Freemasonry is to be in harmony with that, that is harmonious. To be a master mason is to be a child of mankind, a minister of people, a seeker of wisdom, a giver of knowledge. As the master plumber and the master electrician are the ones to hire others, so then is the master mason one to direct men and women in an upward direction if the master mason is just that. All are not masters, though all may be masons in membership. It depends on the digestion of the Masonic meal that was eaten.

Our degrees are such that many years are spent in search of that which was given to each candidate in the very first degree: love of God, love of fellowman. Everything else is just so much trappings. Yet how can you tell intelligent men that is the most profound truth to be found? It is much too simple. So consequently, the mason must search throughout his lifetime to "come right back home" to learn. How wonderful it would be if the master mason could understand this simple lesson that has been taught from time immemorial. But it is not to be, for man is complex and dwells not on simple things. Wisdom has been taken from the wide and the prudent and given to babes. But we, as humans, do not believe that. Therefore, we must work by the sweat of our brow, even in the search for wisdom and knowledge.

In the Masonic fraternity, like all organizations, there is a baby—a baby where wisdom is hidden. The body is the entered apprentice mason; the spirit is the faithful breast. If the entered apprentice mason learns nothing else, Brotherly Love, Relief, and Truth would be enough. If the fellowcraft could sum up the entire lesson of the second degree, it would be to "stand tall, act square, and remember." If the master mason is to master the work, his goal should be Friendship, Morality, and Brotherly Love. All else is outside the square and compasses.

The Highest Degree

This will be the last article in the series, for it will tell of the highest degree in Freemasonry. This will cause some controversy as we have used the term "higher degrees" and the thirty-third and last degree, or the Knights Templar degree as the "highest degree in the York Rite." Those degrees are lateral degrees and are not to be confused with the master mason's degree. For once, you have mastered something; you have made it to the top. However, three degrees do not make you a master, just puts you in position to really get with it!

The master mason is the provider of all members in the Prince Hall Masonic family, and that alone would make it the highest degree, for without him, all others would fall for lack of support, much like a building when the basement is undermined. The master mason outnumbers all other houses of Freemasonry, and it is from the master mason's ranks that we get grand masters, the highest office attainable in the Masonic family. It is well that the grand master holds all other degrees in both rites, York and Scottish, but it is not necessary. We do hold that peace and harmony will prevail much better if all grand masters were not only members of all the houses but active in them. He would truly be a grand master of masons. As stated, it is not necessary that he belongs, but something will be lost in a jurisdiction if it is to the contrary. Time and events have proven this but nuff said about others' business.

The master mason finds that the lesson of the third degree is what makes it the highest, that so spirituality. There is water; there is blood; but spirit gives the journey its purpose, its direction, its loftiness. Without that spirit, man is no more than an animal, a thing. But because of spirit, man is a living soul. Man alone determines his destiny, unless there is divine intervention. While man travels through this "vale of tears," he is at once a creature of responsibility, one that the world's lesser creations look upon as master, one that has subdued the earth. Man has been entrusted with wisdom, the ingredient that lifts him up to the heights of eagles or the knowledge that causes him to think deep, surpassing oceans in depth.

The master mason epitomizes the loftiness of the ideals of the perfect and upright man, yet the man never reaches that perfection here on earth. It is a goal, and the master mason is taught that the goal is reached through the loftiest principles of life, the love of God, the love of man, each bearing its own responsibilities. The master mason should strive to reach this Utopian state, however unattainable it may seem. To not do so is to admit defeat in man's quest to go back to paradise from which he was ejected so many years ago. That spirituality that the master mason seeks in his studies and in his life's doings is the same spirituality that separates us even from angels, giving answer to David's question: "What is man?"

The lesson for the apprentice mason will give us direction, and the lesson of intellect of the fellowcraft mason will give us reason. But it is spirituality that gives us completeness with Him who created us. That spirituality is not easily attained, and many have started out on this journey but didn't make it. It is not ours to say who will and who won't, but it is ours to assist where we can, for that spirituality makes us duty bound to assist and serve wherever and whenever you can. The quest of finding that spirituality in this life is fruitless when viewed as a goal. But if it is taken as a journey, then all of mankind reaps the harvest of noble intentions and lofty ideals and purposes. To seek that spirituality is to travel upward in thought but downward in practice, for that spirit is manifested when you bend over to help lift fallen brethren as exemplified by the five points of fellowship; you go on foot and out of your way to assist and serve. It is manifested when

your brother's welfare is given preference over your own. It is manifested when a brother's character is worth defending, and your own counseling is worth giving even when it is faced with wrongdoing.

The master mason's degree is the highest degree attainable, for what degree could teach you Brotherly Love and Affection. And what higher title could you be called than Brother.

Prince Hall Masonry-Biblical Parallels: Solomon, Worshipful Master

The presiding officers in a Masonic order, as well as the other officers, can find parallels to relate to in the Holy Bible, whether assumed or unauthenticated. This gives purpose and meaning in seeking reasons for certain traditions and peculiar avenues of traveling. Such is the case of the worshipful master representing Solomon.

The master in a lodge represents a pillar of wisdom, one to plan, one to contrive, one to put plans on the trestle board of the lodge. Too often, the master is found doing everything but his job, whatever else it can be said that Solomon was a king, every inch in every way—a righteous king? No, but certainly a king. As was Solomon, the master of a lodge is a man first, then an elected officer in the second greatest order in the world. Since history has dealt with

Solomon's mistakes and travel a different route than those that was taken by the master's counterpart.

As Solomon showed forth wisdom in his everyday decisions concerning life among his people, so should the master show wisdom in his dealings with his charges, the members of his lodge. As the sun gives new life to God's creations, so should the master give new life to the members. As the moon is a beacon in a darkened world, so should the master remember that he is master, both day and night. And like the sun and moon, he should be in equilibrium with the decisions that he must make concerning the lodge's business. While others may sleep, the master should be planning. While others may be playing, the master should be praying. While others may be in disagreement with each other, the master must display justice and fairness in all aspects.

A master is a master 24 hours a day, 7 days a week, 365 days a year, and it can be no other way if success is to be witnessed. Too often, I see masters begin their lodge work on the night of the meeting, and consequently, he is in a hurry and unorganized. I have seen masters have no plan and then wonder why members do not come out to meetings. The answers are very simple: There were no 5 Ps—Prior Planning Prevents Poor Performance. There are too many things that attract our member's minds and attention these days! There are televisions, telephones, other people, football, baseball, basketball, etc. Therefore, we must offer the member something that is at once nourishing yet entertaining; interesting yet attainable, fulfilling yet rewarding. Whether you know it or not, Freemasonry is all of the above. The duties of the master are very clear on the matter: Give them goof and wholesome instructions or cause the same to be done. This little explanation may escape a few ears, but it is very simple: Know what you're doing; know who to get if you don't know what to say, or know who to get to say it; know when to do and say, or know when to postpone.

A master—a smart one that is—knows what the members like by knowing when to listen. Every member knows what he likes, but not every member will tell you. Therefore, the smart master knows himself and, like the saying goes, "to thine own self be true." A master must be first then if he is to be number one. A master is to be in the front if he is to lead. When funds are called for, the master's money should be on the table first. When tickets are issued for sale, the master should take his first and sell the most. B. B. King said it in a song, "You have to pay the cost if you want to be the boss." God forbid for an officer to take up a collection and don't start the collection with his own donation, saying, "Ya'll come!" Who wants to follow a leader that does not lead, and who wants to give to a project that the leader does not believe in? I don't!

Biblical Parallels: Hiram of Tyre, Senior Warden

Hiram, king of Tyre, was a good friend of David, king of Israel, and was destined to go down in history as the conveyor of support in the history of the Masonic order. No matter how good a plan, if there is no support for it, it all stands for naught. Therefore, the worshipful master and the senior warden should be good friends. One is to look good now, while the other is to follow later.

Tyre was a seafaring nation, giving us the ancient Phoenicians and Carthaginians that plied the oceans of the world in trade missions that stands as a pattern today. In the history of David, Hiram promised David anything in the way of help that he would need in exchange for cities and other concessions. However, David had the blood of Uriah the Hittite on his hands, and the building of the temple of God would rest in David's son Solomon's hands. This would mean that Solomon had everything together because of the work of his father, David. Many times in our lives, plans were set forth long before we came on the scene. Sacrifices were made; promises were made; and treaties were signed, all because of friendship.

Tyre was also noted for its craftsmen, men of cunning and great skills in dyes, especially purple, the cloth of royalty. In Tyre were stone setters, commonly called masons today. The Tyrians artisans were needed, for the Israelites could only build mud huts, and the temple of God must be a masterpiece. The Tyrians knew of the tall Cedars of Lebanon, those legendary trees that grew as far down as they did up, trees that had roots to grow through rocks rather than around them. Solomon would furnish the hewers of trees, but it would be Hiram of Tyre to furnish the craftsmen to show the Hebrews how to cut and square trees and stones. The trees would be cut in Lebanon and then floated up to the port of Joppa and, thence, overland to Jerusalem. It would take a people that knew of the Mediterranean Sea's current to do this, and the Phoenician sailors were the best. They knew of the undercurrent that would more or less sail against the current; seemingly others did not know of the strong undercurrent that caused the rafts of cedar trees to float up steam to Joppa.

A good support system is strength to a plan, and Hiram was emblematical of that strength, and we recognize him in the Doric column of the Greeks, a pillar of brute strength, complimenting the ionic column of Solomon's wisdom. Because of the support given to Solomon by Hiram, king of Tyre, and certainly by Almighty God, the temple was completed in just under seven years. During this time, God showed his support in the venture by not allowing it to rain in the daytime. Solomon showed his wisdom by having the stones drawn, squared, and numbered in the quarry, some miles from the temple site. No sound of axe or hammer or nail or anything metallic was heard at the temple site in those seven years.

Hiram showed his support even further by loaning Solomon a namesake. Hiram Abiff, a widow's son of Tyre, a Hebrew from the tribe of Naphtali. A successful venture does not always have leaders out front. Sometimes, another is called upon to show forth beauty, and this is just what Hiram Abiff had to offer. For fear of getting into the next article, we will leave Hiram Abiff alone for now and concentrate on Hiram the king.

Physical support is important, but one cannot do without spiritual support. Hiram of Tyre had both to give to Solomon mainly because of David, Solomon's father. Many times, we are blessed because of our fathers or mothers, not for ourselves. Solomon was not given wisdom for his sake. God's covenant had been with David coming down through the tribe of Judah. Therefore, since David was dead, Hiram turned that love of David toward Solomon, and because of it, Solomon's temple was completed.

Biblical Parallels: Hiram Abiff, Junior Warden

As the sun in the south, at its meridian height, is the glory and the beauty of the day, so stands the junior warden in the south. Those words are familiar to all Freemasons as part of the opening ceremonies of a masonic lodge. Whether it is understood or not is another thing. Hiram Abiff, as a character in the overall story of Freemasonry, probably is misunderstood too, for his story is an allusion of a greater and more devout truth than what meets the eye.

When the sun is as its zenith or meridian height, man is contained in all his glory, casting no shadow, creating no false image. Hiram's job was to beautify King Solomon's temple in Jerusalem. Being a native of Tyre, he was greatly familiar with the intricacies of purples, brass, and stonework. As an expert in the field, he was considered a grand master in ancient legends about the building of the temple, given charge of the entered apprenticed masons. What wisdom was to the contriving of the plans for the temple. What strength was to support the undertaking. Hiram is Beauty, the adorning of the temple. A greater beauty came not through the temple but through the legendary coming together of two sets of masons, the operative and the speculative. Two sets of lives came together in a project of cooperation that became an avenue of sharing with each other—one to build, the other to live right.

Hiram Abiff was an added attraction, displaying the friendship of Hiram the king toward David, the king of Israel. He was sent to put the finishing touches on a marvelous accomplishment, the temple that would house the Almighty. The building was to be a wonder itself. But through Hiram Abiff's work and cunning, it became a model for all places of worship in the world, even to this day. Then too, it was not all Hiram, for God had put down the pattern at creation, and all Hiram had to do was follow the pattern handed down from God through Solomon. The temple would take on the characteristics of man, stating to generations to come, how it is in the universe. All one would have to do is look at his fellowman. Hiram put two pillars before the outer porch, Boaz and Jachin, just as God put two natures in man—one physical, one spiritual. Hiram put twelve gates about the temple; man has four limbs with three joints in each. The temple had three places in it, the outer porch, the holy place, the most holy place. Man has blood, water, and spirit, witnessed by the abdominal cavities, chest cavities, and skull or brain cavity.

Each section of the temple meant something for the good of mankind, a lesson in theology, as well as theosophy. History was written in stone, the mark of a mason, depicting the trials of the Israelites as they traveled through the wilderness of Zin, per the two pillars at the entrance. These two pillars at the entrance. These pillars let them know of fire and water, the two saving elements in the desert as they traveled for forty years—fire that led them by night and water that led them by day. This emblematical lesson would be repeated on the banks of the Jordan River as John proclaimed that "I baptize with water, but one comes after me that baptizes with the Holy Ghost, and with fire...as he increases, I must decrease." As God became more manifested in the hearts of righteous men, the need for a building, such as Solomon's Temple, decreased. The spiritual increased over the physical.

Hiram Abiff's cunning worked for the temple when he went to the clay grounds between Succoth and Zeredatha where he cast all the vessels for the temple. His knowledge of gold and brass was rewarding as he made all the basins, the altars, the candlesticks, the pomegranates, the lily work, the twelve brazen oxen, holding up the universe, which we know today as the zodiac and as the twelve tribes of Israel. His expertise in all manner of cunning work was well-thought-of by Solomon. So it is in the lodge with the junior warden when the craft is at refreshment.

About the Author

Larry joined the Masonic Organization in 1982 and had held various positions in the Masonic organization. Larry studied under the Howard Woods's the Grand Master of Arkansas for two years. Larry received all of his houses before graduating college in 1984, Scottish Rite and York Rite. Became a Shriner in 1987 and a thirty-third in 2004. Larry has traveled the world in masonry, stateside and overseas, where still he found a brother to be a Brother in masonry. Larry attempted to thank Howard Woods before he passed for the lesson that he gave him at a young age. Howard said, "If you really want to thank me, Pass It On." That is why you have this book from his papers and teaching.